SOS to Encode!

Part 1

An Intensive, Multisensory Reading, Spelling and Writing Program

Josh Morgan, M.A.Ed.

Literacy Specialist
Special Educator
Intervention Coach (MTSS/PBIS)

SOS to Encode!
An Intensive, Multisensory Reading, Spelling, and Writing Program
Part 1

SOS to Encode! is a series of scaffolded, instructional programs designed to address the need for quality, research-based, convenient tools to improve writing ability. Each part of the series uses multisensory strategies to build encoding, phonics, and sentence editing skills.

SOS to Encode! provides:
- ❖ Placement tests to determine exact instructional intensity needed for students and groups
- ❖ Three levels of intensity and rates of instruction
- ❖ Ongoing formative assessments to monitor progress
- ❖ Multisensory phonics techniques
- ❖ Multiple visual cues and mnemonic devices to support spelling and editing skills
- ❖ Developmentally scaffolded phonics and encoding skills

SOS to Encode! Part 1 strategies:
- ❖ The "COPS" self-monitoring strategy
  - ➢ Capitalization, Overall Appearance, Punctuation, Spelling
  - ➢ Visual Supports (e.g. bookmarks, posters, etc.)
- ❖ Decoding strategies
  - ➢ Segment and blend phonemes to write and to check spelling
- ❖ Encoding strategies
  - ➢ Modified Simultaneous Oral Spelling technique
    - ▪ Finger Tapping Phonemes
    - ▪ Table Pounding Sentences
    - ▪ Spelling Aloud

By the end of Part 1 of the SOS Program, students will be able to:
- ❖ Encode, decode, and spell one-, two-, and three-syllable words that include:
  - ➢ Closed Syllables
  - ➢ Short Vowels
  - ➢ Consonant Digraphs
- ❖ Check writing for correct sentence mechanics following independent writing
- ❖ Self-monitor writing during the writing process
- ❖ Recognize and spell non-decodable words

Table of Contents

Visit this site to download color visuals and the supplemental data sheets listed below:

https://www.joshmorganconsulting.com/sostoencode
(Password: sos2017)

Formative Assessments   Class wide Instructional Schedule
Class Pre- & Post-Test Record   Weekly Instructional Distribution

This program is designed to support the reading and writing development of early readers, students in early primary grades, at-risk students, and those with special or language needs. The design of the program is an effort to address encoding difficulties in the early primary grade while also ensuring the development of a flexible, intensive, user-friendly tool. This program is intended to supplement the core-reading program by providing multisensory encoding strategies, a systematic sound-symbol correspondence structure, and self-monitoring mnemonics for sentence mechanics. While Kindergarten and first grade teachers may find the strategies to be effective for Tier 1 instruction, this is not a program that you will need to fully implement with every student, and is not meant to be used throughout the entire school year. It should be used as a tool to remediate or teach encoding skills, determine student level of need, and to build writing ability in struggling students.

Materials and Structure:

The *SOS to Encode!* series has been designed to provide three levels of intensity within each part of the program based on the current ability of each student. The placement test is recommended for all students in class as a screening tool, and is an easy way to group students with the highest need for encoding instruction. The placement test allows instruction to focus on the needs of a single student or small group of students. A series of recommendations accompany the placement tests to guide instructional decision making and planning. The assessment also serves as a Pre- and Post-Test to allow the teacher to measure growth, organize placement recommendations, and group students homogeneously. Using the Pre- and Post-Test with all students in the classroom can afford a wealth of growth data on spelling and sentence mechanics for students receiving this intervention, other interventions, and/or the Tier 1 program. Further analysis of this data could prompt rich discussions comparing Tier 1 growth with each encoding intervention to determine which is closing the skill gap more effectively.

Rationale:

The debate between whole language instruction and skills based instruction has spurred many changes in classroom instruction for teachers across the nation. Teachers learn about whole language instruction (i.e. Guided Reading, Soar to Success, etc.) in professional development courses and are encouraged to use authentic, student-centered activities to promote independence and intrinsic motivations for students. Yet, when teachers attempt to support independence and creative expression, specific skills-based instruction is often lacking in the daily routine of their students. Skills-based direct instruction is, too often, addressed solely through word work or whole group instruction a few times each week. This instruction on specific skills is rarely systematic or formatively assessed consistently, to ensure that all students are mastering the phonics and sentence writing skills. Without this systematic assessment and remediation, instructional gaps compound with each year. The students who are able to adapt and learn excel, while students who need a strong focus on explicit phonics instruction and maintenance programs continue to struggle. When students are unable to read and write effectively on daily assignments and summative assessments, this instigates pressure from parents and school administrators to focus on skills, and less on creativity, further perpetuating this dichotomy. Often this pressure is placed on teachers in upper grades who do not have years of experience and training in teaching basic encoding and decoding skills.

This program integrates systematic, multisensory writing instruction and the "C.O.P.S." sentence editing strategy (Lienemann & Reid, 2006) into the daily classroom routine of struggling students throughout elementary school. The integration of multisensory, sentence dictation and editing practices provide experience, support, and encouragement to utilize appropriate writing conventions and strategies when writing spontaneously.

This program and many others are based on the multisensory reading and writing methodology provided in <u>The Gillingham Manual: Remedial Training for Children with Specific Disability in Reading, Spelling, and Penmanship</u> (Gillingham & Stillman, 1997). The foundation of these programs is a systematic reading and writing structure along with effective strategies to build phoneme retention, phoneme segmentation, phoneme blending, sight word retention, sentence mechanics, and editing. However, this program offers specific, intensive short-term instruction for struggling students to build the skills needed to access the Tier 1 curriculum. Gillingham and Stillman used "Simultaneous Oral Spelling" (S.O.S.) to "firmly establish the visual-auditory-kinesthetic linkages or associations (Gillingham & Stillman, 1997, p. 35)." This encourages retention of sound-symbol correspondences. The strategy includes the teacher saying the word, students echoing the word, segmenting the word, and writing the letters (naming each letters as it is formed). This strategy stresses phonetics to attempt unknown word and provides visual prompts to include accurate spellings of non-decodable words until they are no longer needed. Once students are able to engage in S.O.S. to write words, sentence dictation begins using multisensory activities (pounding out words) and a research-based editing strategy, "C.O.P.S."

Content:

Dictation

Writing dictation has been a focus of various researchers attempting to determine the effectiveness of specific interventions and problem solving strategies to support students who struggle with reading and writing for various reasons. This research supports the need for student-centered activities to build student confidence and motivation. Many students need remediation in sentence writing and explicit instruction on the structure and mechanics of sentences. Observations in primary classrooms have garnered evidence that while many students enjoy writing independently, they often become frustrated when they do not yet have the skills to write a sentence or spell the words they are trying to write. This struggle compounds over the elementary years as these deficits remain.

Simultaneous Oral Spelling

Research on the use of "Simultaneous Oral Spelling"(SOS) and multisensory instruction (i.e. the Visual-Auditory-Kinesthetic-Tactile method) offers a wealth of evidence that this could be an effective strategy to build phoneme retention and sentence writing ability (Long, et al., 2007; Mee, 1998; Benton, 1998). The strategies detailed in The Gillingham Manual (Gillingham & Stillman, 1997) provide a structure for the use of SOS in the dictation of words and sentences. The manual presents the use of SOS in the structure of a "Four Point Program" which delivers consistent multisensory strategies to assist encoding (Gillingham & Stillman, 1997, p. 35).

Self-monitoring with Sentence Mechanics

At all levels of writing, it is essential to be able to monitor the one's writing process and revise for correctness and readability. The use of the "COPS" editing strategy is supported by research on ten self-regulating strategies (MacArthur, et al., 2006). The strategy additionally focuses on ensuring self-efficacy, confidence, and student control during spontaneous, independent writing experiences.

Analysis of Pertinent Research

Recent research studies conducted on student self-regulation and the use of mnemonic strategies support the use of strategies and training to generalize skills to untaught examples (Abner-Morgan, et al., 2007; Gore, 2002; Lienemann & Reid, 2006; Westwood, 2008). According to the research, the use of direct instruction and the specific targeting of writing skills encourages fluency, automaticity, and generalization of the skill.

Abner-Morgan, Hessler, and Konrad (2007), support the practice of direct instruction and targeting specific skills to ensure generalization of the skills to novel examples. The researchers discuss the use of the "general case strategy" coined by Homer, Williams, and Stevely (1987) when referring to the practice of systematically providing varied examples of experiences practicing the strategy to build mastery and generalization of the strategy. The utilization of effecting teaching examples "can be developed after examining all variations of the target skill required in each generalization setting" (Alber-Morgan, et al., 2007). Research conducted by Gore (2002), supports the use of teaching examples and scaffolding in studies using "bare bones" sentences to build student ability to read and writing paragraphs.

The research of Alber-Morgan, et al. (2007) also supports student use of checklists when revising and editing writing to develop their ability to categorize each type of error and to ensure they search their writing for each category (p. 119). The researchers go on to support the use of acronyms or mnemonics to encourage memorization of these checklists in order to generalize their ability to find errors to situations where the checklist is not available. The use of the "COPS" acronym to remind students to search through their writing piece for errors based on four categories: capitalization, overall appearance, punctuation, and spelling are one of several available to provide this type of instructional support.

Gibson (2003) and Lienemann & Reid (2006) conducted research into the use of mnemonic strategies to encourage fluency of skills. Gore's (2003) research with building the memory of deaf students further established that, "The importance of rehearsal, repetition, and mnemonics are identified as key memory developing strategies" (p. 30). Mnemonic devices are used to associate unknown material with familiar experiences. This, in turn, relieves short-term memory effort because retrieval is possible with a single association grounded in already existing code in the long-term memory. The development of these strategies builds memory, making it possible for fluent recollection and use of learned skills. When participants were taught mnemonic strategies, they recalled the information with greater speed and accuracy.

Program Components:

Pre-Post Tests and Placement Test: The two assessments, Sentence Dictation and the Open-Ended Spontaneous Writing Sample are used as both Pre-, Post- and Placement Assessments.

Sentence Dictation:

- Pre Test: Provides a baseline for sentence mechanics.
- Post Test: Offers a measure of growth at the end of the program and informs next steps.
- Diagnostic: Allows teachers to note error patterns to determine which of the four skills will provide the highest level of frustration for the student(s). Teachers can then provide a stronger focus on these skills (i.e. capitalization, spelling, etc.).

Open-Ended Spontaneous Writing Sample:

- Pre Test: Assigns a writing stage to the work sample of each student prior to beginning the program. This provides an initial baseline to be used to determine growth.
- Post Test: Offers information concerning student growth by assigning a final writing stage at the conclusion of the program. Students may need additional practice formulating sentences.
- Diagnostic: Provides information concerning student writing stages (e.g. scribbling, development of letters and letter like shapes, writing known, isolated words, etc.). This assessment, while less sensitive to growth than the Sentence Dictation Assessment, allows teachers to focus on skills needed to move from one stage to the next.

Placement Recommendations

Both assessments, when used in conjunction with the placement recommendations chart, allow teachers to group and place students in the program.

Program Components:

Pre-Post Tests and Placement Test:

The program offers two types of data sheets to record scores and recommendations from the Pre-Test: an individual student record and a class-wide record. Samples of each data sheet are included for guidance.

Individual Student Pre / Post Assessment Record Sheet:

Provides a single form to collect pre- and post-assessment data for both the open-ended and sentence dictation assessment. Growth data and missing skills are also collected.

Class Pre-Post Test Record (download on website)

The class wide data sheet provides an organized tool for recording all pre- and post-assessment data. Teachers are asked to write in the action following each assessment (e.g. Plan A, Plan B, Plan C, or Test Part 2). Teachers also categorize each student into up to six homogenous groups based on student achievement on the Pre-Test (i.e. Very High, High, Medium, Low Medium, Low, and Very Low). Group distribution data is collected to the right of the sheet. This provides class wide information about the number of students in each group during the pre- and post-assessments and helps to determine if students are moving to higher-level skills and groups. A simple, user-friendly section at the bottom of the sheet guides the teacher in analyzing the pre- and post-test quickly.

Program Components:

Formative Assessments (download on website)

To record data from formative assessments completed at the end of each lesson (dictation sheet), two data sheets are provided at the individual and small group level. Samples follow each form to guide your assessments and recommendations.

Individual Student Formative Assessment Record

The individual formative assessment record provides ongoing progress tracking data for each student. The form provides an opportunity to assess student growth, determine need, and collect growth data on specific skills that include decodable words, sight words, capitalization, organization, punctuation, and spelling. There is also space to include next steps following each lesson. This form is the perfect tool to use when sharing progress data with families at parent conferences or data review meetings.

Small Group: Weekly Formative Assessment Record

The small group data sheet for formative assessments provides a record for up to six students in a group. Placement data, formative assessment data, and recommendations are recorded. Placement test data and plan is recorded at the top of the sheet along with space for additional assessments. Prior to beginning lessons, the teacher records placement data and student names, assigning a letter (A-F) to each student. After completing the dictation sheet with the group, the teacher records: lesson number, lesson date, assessment data (decodable words, sight words, and sentence mechanics), and number of students that met mastery, and next steps (whether to move the student to the next lesson, repeat lesson, and what to skill to focus on specifically during the next lesson).

Program Components:

Class wide, Small-Group Instructional Schedule and Instructional Distribution

The instructional schedule and weekly instructional distribution are optional but can assist in guiding the integration of the SOS program into your reading rotation.

Class wide, Small-Group Instructional Schedule (download on website)

The top chart allows the teacher to schedule small group reading instruction during the reading block. You may choose to incorporate SOS into your writing block as well.

There are four rotations provided for each day of the week. Each group is usually 20-25 minutes in duration but may vary based on your classroom schedule and Tier 1 instructional program. Groups for SOS are determined by pre-assessments while the groups for the Tier 1 program (Guided Reading in the sample) will be determined by classroom assessments. You will notice that the schedule is organized to ensure five days of small group instruction, both SOS and Guided Reading, for the neediest students. The teacher fills in the times for each rotation at the top of each column. To schedule, the rest of the boxes are filled in with the program and the group level in each box corresponding to the specific weekday and time.

Class wide, Small Group Instructional Schedule   TEACHER:_____   GRADE:____   YEAR:_____
Based Pre-Post Group Schedule

High and Very High (7 Students): Run Tier 1 Reading and Writing and Retest

READING ROTATIONS				
	Time:	Time:	Time:	Time:
Monday				
Tuesday				
Wednesday				
Thursday				
Friday				

GR: Guided Reading   Other:_____   Other:_____
SOS: Simultaneous Oral Spelling   Other:_____   Other:_____

Weekly Instructional Distribution (download on website)

A quick tool to determine your weekly instructional distribution is included at the bottom of the form. This is used to monitor the amount of small group instruction each group receives. The students who need more intensive instruction receive more instruction that more independent peers.

Small Group: Weekly Instructional Distribution(number of groups per week listed)

	Guided Reading	SOS-dictation	Total Literacy Small Groups Each Week
Very High			
High			
Mid			
Low Mid			
Low			
Very Low			

Program Components:

Session and Lesson Plan Structure

Consistency in the multisensory strategies is critical to the success of this program. The Session Lesson Plan Structure provides a detailed, explicit process for both Remediation and Treatment.

Remedial Instruction: Introduction to SOS/ Multisensory Procedures

The remedial lessons (Lesson 1 and 2) may be repeated as needed until students gain facility with the SOS strategies. Mastery of these skills is imperative to the success of the program. Expected times are provided to keep the lesson plan on track. Remember the lesson can be repeated if students are unable to move on using the formative assessment.

Treatment: Simultaneous Oral Spelling

After Lesson Two all lessons are based on the treatment lesson plan structure. Each SOS lesson structure is identical and uses the same procedure. The accompanying Instructional Framework and Lesson Materials provide the decodable words, sight words, and sentences for each lesson.

The multisensory protocols used when encoding include:

- Phonetic Words,
- Sight Words, and
- Sentences.

Remedial Instruction: Introduction to SOS & Multisensory procedures

1. SOS – Phonemes (5 minutes)
   1. Teacher says/shows phoneme
   2. Students repeat phoneme
   3. If correct, students write letter in sand as they say name
   4. Student repeats phoneme and name
2. SOS- phonetic words (10 minutes)
   1. Teacher says/shows word
   2. Students repeat word
   3. Students segment the sounds
   4. Students spell word aloud
   5. If correct, students write letters as they say names
   6. Student reads the word.
3. SOS – sight words (10 minutes)
   1. Teacher says/shows word
   2. Students repeat word
   3. Students "tap out" word and repeat.
   4. Students spell word aloud
   5. If correct, students write letters as they say names
   6. Student reads the word.
4. Introduce multisensory sentence segmentation (5 minutes)
   1. Teacher says sentence
   2. Teacher "pounds out sentence"
   3. Students and teacher "pound out" sentence
   4. Students "pound out" sentences.
   5. Repeat with each sentence.

Treatment: Simultaneous Oral Spelling (SOS)

1. SOS- phonetic words/detached syllables (5 minutes)
   a. Teacher says/shows word/syllable
   b. Students repeat word
   c. Students segment the sounds (finger tap)
   d. Students spell word aloud
   e. If correct, students write letters as they say names
   f. Student decodes the word.

2. SOS – sight words (5 minutes)
   a. Teacher says/shows word
   b. Students repeat word
   c. Students finger tap letter names of word and repeat.
   d. Students spell word aloud
   e. If correct, students write letters as they say names
   f. Student reads the word.

3. SOS sentences (10-20 minutes)
   a. Teacher says/shows sentence
   b. Students repeat sentence
   c. Students segment (table pound) sentence
   d. Based on word type students:
      - finger tap phonemes (decodable word)
      - or finger tap letter names (sight word)
   e. Students spell word aloud
   f. If correct, students write letters as they say names
   g. Student reads the word.
   h. Repeat appropriate technique with each word.
   i. Student reads sentence.
   j. Students use COPS to edit sentence and correct based on model sentence.
   k. 1st Lesson: Fully Guided Editing
   l. 2nd Lesson: Guide only when needed
   Repeat with each sentence.

Program Components:

Instructional Framework and Common Core Connections

The Instructional Framework provides a Scope and Sequence for the program while the Common Core Connections align specific lessons to standards.

Instructional Framework

The framework includes specific information for each lesson and includes number of words in dictated sentences, lesson format (Remedial or SOS), sentences, CVC words, sight words, and phonemes. Bloom and Traub developed the phoneme order, decodable words, and sentences in Recipe for Reading: Intervention Strategies for Struggling Readers (2005). The words in each lesson utilize mastered phonemes from previous lessons to ensure student success. This allows the teacher to include word and sentence writing practice prior to students becoming fluent with all phonemes.

SOS to Encode! Part 1   **Instructional Framework**

Adapted from Bloom & Traub, 2005

Lesson	# of words in dictated sentences	Lesson Format	Sentences for dictation / segmenting	Words for SOS/ cards			Focus phonemes
				Focus CVC	Supplemental CVC	Sight Word	
1	1	Remedial	Go doc go! The cat is bad. The dog is mad. We play. We run.	cad cod doc	dad dac ad od	a go I	c, o, a, d
2	1	Remedial	Segmenting: The dog is mad. The house is pretty. I can play outside.	dog mad dam	cog lad hog ham had	see the is	g, m, h, l
3	2	SOS	Tom got. Dot had. Tim did.	tag Tim hit	hot lit hid	and me look	t, i
4	2	SOS	Jim hid. Kim did. Kid hit.	jam Kim kit	kid Jim jog	my no play	j, k

Common Core Connections

The Common Core Connections present a list of Common Core Standards for Kindergarten and First grade for each lesson.

SOS to Encode! Part 1   **Common Core Connections**

Lesson #	Kindergarten	First Grade
1-2	RF.K.1.B: words are sequences of letters RF.K.1.D: Recognize upper/lower letters RF.K.2.C: blend and segment onset/rime RF.K.2.D: isolate sounds in CVC RF.K.3.A: 1 to 1 letter-sound correspondence RF.K.3.C: read high frequency words	RF.1.2.B: blend phonemes to produce words RF.1.2.C: isolate sounds in CVC RF.1.2.D: segment phonemes RF.1.3.B: decode one syllable words RF.1.3.G: read irregularly spelled words
	In addition to above standards:	**In addition to above standards:**
3-16	RF.K.1.A: follow words left-right, top-bottom RF.K.1.C: words separated by spaces	RF.1.1.A: features of sentence
	In addition to above standards:	**In addition to above standards:**
6, 10-11, 15-16	(no digraph standards in Kindergarten)	RF.1.3.A: spell/decode consonant digraphs

13

Program Components:

Lesson Materials: Each lesson includes a Lesson Guide, Flashcards, and the SOS Dictation Sheet. For teacher convenience, the materials have been condensed into user-friendly implements.

Lesson Guide

Each Lesson Guide is presented in a single page format and includes the focus phoneme(s) or phonics pattern, decodable words, sight words, and sentences. Teachers can share this with families to encourage generalization to homework.

**There is no SOS form for the first two lessons. The Lesson Structure provides remediation to develop the multisensory strategies before engaging in writing.

Flash Cards:

Flash cards for each phoneme, word, and sentence accompany each lesson. Flashcard size is consistent across all lessons to allow easy organization of teacher materials. Teachers can send home copies of flashcards for homework or each student can have their own set of flashcards on a ring.

SOS Dictation Sheet

The SOS Dictation Sheet serves as practice for writing decodable words, sight words, and sentences. The teacher uses SOS with each section. After writing the first sentence, students write a circle in the corresponding box on the "COPS" chart (in the left side of the box). They check place a checkmark in these circles when they correct their error. This is repeated for the second sentence on the right side of each box.

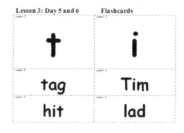

Program Components:

Sentence Mechanics, Self-Monitoring Visual

The "COPS" sentence mechanics strategy is implemented in the program as a consistent, structured, process for self-monitoring sentence mechanics. The visual below can be used as a poster or given to each student for use while editing sentences. Students are able to use the visual during their formative assessments.

Placement Recommendations (Pre-Test)

Open Ended Writing	Sentence Dictation		Pre-Test Recommended Action		
Writing Stage	**Accuracy Range**	**Accuracy Percentage**	**Pre-Test Grouping**	**Pre-Test Action Plan**	**Recommended Program**
1-4	**Begin Fine Motor Instruction**		Focus on letter and word encoding prior to assessing placement in program.		
5-8	**Low: 0-49%**	0-25%	Very Low	**Follow Plan A:** Full Program	SOS to Encode! *Part 1*
		26-50%	Low		
	Mid: 50-75%	51-62%	Low Mid	**Follow Plan B:** Full Phonics Review	SOS to Encode! *Part 1*
		63-75%	Mid		
	High: 76-88%	76-88%	High	**Follow Plan C:** Sentence Mechanics Review	SOS to Encode! *Part 1*
9-10	**Very High: 89-100%**	89-100%	Very High	Conduct **SOS to Encode!** *Part 2* Placement Test	Use SOS to Encode! *Part 2*

Plan A: **Full Program**	Plan B: **Full Phonics Review**	Plan C: **Sentence Mechanics Review**	
Begin Day 1 and run the program as it is. **Each day repeats** to encourage familiarity, fluency, and mastery. Post Test when complete and Follow New Placement Recommendations	Begin Day 1 and run the program spending only a single day on each lesson. Post Test when complete and Follow New Placement Recommendations	**Day**	**Lesson Number**
		1	1
		2	1
		3	2
		4	2
		5	3
		6	5
		7	7
		8	9
		9	11
		10	12
Duration: Days: 32 Weeks: 6-7	**Duration:** Days: 16 Weeks: 3-4	**Duration:** Days: 10 Weeks: 2	

Sentence Dictation   **Circle One:** Pre Test   Post Test
SOS PART 1

Student Directions;
Listen and write the sentences.

Name: _____   Date: _____

1. _____

2. _____

3. _____

4. _____

5. _____

Open Ended Writing   **Circle One:** Pre Test   Post Test
SOS PART 1

Student Directions:
Listen and write about anything you want.

Name: _____   Date: _____

Pre / Post Assessment Record Sheet   Student Name: _____

SENTENCE DICTATION   Skills assessed: Use of Sentence Mechanics, Spelling

Pre Test								
Sentence:	Capitalization		Organization (spaces, on line)		Punctuation		Spelling	
1: Tom got.	0	1	0	1	0	1	0	1
2: Tad got mad.	0	1	0	1	0	1	0	1
3: Jim hid the jam.	0	1	0	1	0	1	0	1
4: It is fun to win.	0	1	0	1	0	1	0	1
5: Tom had a yen to run.	0	1	0	1	0	1	0	1
Total Accurate	/5		/5		/5		/5	
Total Score	/20		**Total Percentage**				%	
Post Test								
Sentence:	Capitalization		Organization (spaces, on line)		Punctuation		Spelling	
1. Dad got.	0	1	0	1	0	1	0	1
2. Dot is sad.	0	1	0	1	0	1	0	1
3. The yam is big.	0	1	0	1	0	1	0	1
4. Tim and his cat run.	0	1	0	1	0	1	0	1
5. A web is on that bed.	0	1	0	1	0	1	0	1
Total Accurate	/5		/5		/5		/5	
Total Score	/20		**Total Percentage**				%	

Quantitative checklist for assessment of writing dictated sentences (Linemann & Reid, 2006)]

OPEN ENDED, SPONTANEOUS WRITING   Skills assessed: Developmental Writing Stage

	Evidence/Stage of Writing	Is this stage evident? Mark an "X" to designate evidence	
		Pre-test	**Post-test**
1	Scribbling		
2	Differentiation between drawing and writing		
3	Concepts of linearity, uniformity, left to right motion		
4	Development of letters and letter like shapes		
5	Combination of letters, possibly with spaces indicating letters, words, and sentences		
6	Writing known, isolated words		
7	Writing simple sentences with use of inventive spellings		
8	Combining two or more sentences to express complete thoughts		
9	Control of punctuation – periods, capitalization, use of upper- and lower-case letters		
10	Form of discourse – stories, information materials, letters, etc.		

Qualitative checklist for open-ended, spontaneous writing assessment. Deford (1991)

Pre-Post Test Analysis

	Sentence Mechanics		Open Ended, Spontaneous Writing Sample
	Main Skill Need	**Score**	**Stage (Number)**
Pre Test		%	
Post Test		%	
Growth		%	

Pre / Post Assessment Record Sheet　　　**Student Name:** _____Sample_____

SENTENCE DICTATION　　　Skills assessed: Use of Sentence Mechanics, Spelling

Pre Test

Sentence:	Capitalization	Organization (spaces, on line)	Punctuation	Spelling
1: Tom got.	0　①	0　①	0　①	0　①
2: Tad got mad.	0　①	0　①	0　①	⓪　1
3: Jim hid the jam.	0　1	0　①	0　①	⓪　1
4: It is fun to win.	0　①	0　①	0　①	⓪　1
5: Tom had a yen to run.	0　1	0　①	0　①	⓪　1
Total Accurate	3/5	5/5	5/5	1/5
Total Score	14/20	**Total Percentage**		70%

Post Test

Sentence:	Capitalization	Organization (spaces, on line)	Punctuation	Spelling
1. Dad got.	0　①	0　①	0　①	0　①
2. Dot is sad.	0　①	0　①	0　①	0　①
3. The yam is big.	0　①	0　①	0　①	0　①
4. Tim and his cat run.	0　①	0　①	0　①	0　①
5. A web is on that bed.	0　①	0　①	0　①	⓪　1
Total Accurate	5/5	5/5	5/5	4/5
Total Score	19 / 20	**Total Percentage**		95%

Quantitative checklist for assessment of writing dictated sentences (Linemann & Reid, 2006)]

OPEN ENDED, SPONTANEOUS WRITING　　　Skills assessed: Developmental Writing Stage

	Evidence/Stage of Writing	Is this stage evident? Mark an "X" to designate evidence	
		Pre-test	**Post-test**
1	Scribbling	X	X
2	Differentiation between drawing and writing	X	X
3	Concepts of linearity, uniformity, left to right motion	X	X
4	Development of letters and letter like shapes	X	X
5	Combination of letters, possibly with spaces indicating letters, words, and sentences	X	X
6	Writing known, isolated words	X	X
7	Writing simple sentences with use of inventive spellings	X	X
8	Combining two or more sentences to express complete thoughts		
9	Control of punctuation – periods, capitalization, use of upper- and lower-case letters		
10	Form of discourse – stories, information materials, letters, etc.		

Qualitative checklist for open-ended, spontaneous writing assessment. Deford (1991)

Pre-Post Test Analysis

	Sentence Mechanics		Open Ended, Spontaneous Writing Sample
	Main Skill Need	**Score**	**Stage (Number)**
Pre Test	Spelling	70%	7
Post Test	Spelling	95%	7
Growth		25%	0

Remedial Instruction: Introduction to SOS & Multisensory procedures	Treatment: Simultaneous Oral Spelling (SOS)

1. <u>SOS – Phonemes (5 minutes)</u>
1. Teacher says/shows phoneme
2. Students repeat phoneme
3. If correct, students write letter in sand as they say name
4. Student repeats phoneme and name.
 	
2. <u>SOS- phonetic words (10 minutes)</u>
1. Teacher says/shows word
2. Students repeat word
3. Students segment the sounds
4. Students spell word aloud
5. If correct, students write letters as they say names
6. Student reads the word.
 	
3. <u>SOS – sight words (10 minutes)</u>
1. Teacher says/shows word
2. Students repeat word
3. Students "tap out" word and repeat.
4. Students spell word aloud
5. If correct, students write letters as they say names
6. Student reads the word.
 	
4. <u>Introduce multisensory sentence segmentation (5 minutes)</u>
1. Teacher says sentence
2. Teacher "pounds out sentence"
3. Students and teacher "pound out" sentence
4. Students "pound out" sentences.
5. Repeat with each sentence.
	1. <u>SOS- phonetic words/detached syllables (5 minutes)</u>
	a. Teacher says/shows word/syllable
	b. Students repeat word
	c. Students segment the sounds **(finger tap)**
	d. Students spell word aloud
	e. If correct, students write letters as they say names
	f. Student decodes the word.
	
	2. <u>SOS – sight words (5 minutes)</u>
	a. Teacher says/shows word
	b. Students repeat word
	c. Students **finger tap** letter names of word and repeat.
	d. Students spell word aloud
	e. If correct, students write letters as they say names
	f. Student reads the word.
	
	3. <u>SOS sentences (10-20 minutes)</u>
	a. Teacher says/shows sentence
	b. Students repeat sentence
	c. Students segment **(table pound)** sentence
	d. Based on word type students:
	   • **finger tap** phonemes (decodable word)
	   • or **finger tap** letter names (sight word)
	e. Students spell word aloud
	f. If correct, students write letters as they say names
	g. Student reads the word.
	h. Repeat appropriate technique with each word.
	i. Student reads sentence.
	j. Students use COPS to edit sentence and correct based on model sentence
	k. 1st Lesson: Fully Guided Editing
	l. 2nd Lesson: Guide only when needed
	   Repeat with each sentence.

SOS to Encode! Part 1　　　**Instructional Framework**

Adapted from Bloom & Traub, 2005

Lesson	# of words in dictated sentences	Lesson Format	Sentences for dictation / segmenting	Words for SOS/ cards			Focus phonemes
				Focus CVC	Supplemental CVC	Sight Word	
1	1	Remedial	Go doc go! The cat is bad. The dog is mad. We play. We run.	cad cod doc	dad dac ad od	a go I	c, o, a, d
2	1	Remedial	**Segmenting:** The dog is mad. The house is pretty. I can play outside.	dog mad dam	cog lad hog ham had	see the is	g, m, h, l
3	2	SOS	Tom got. Dot had. Tim did.	tag Tim hit	hot lit hid	and me look	t, i
4	2	SOS	Jim hid. Kim did. Kid hit.	jam Kim kit	kid Jim jog	my no play	j, k
5	3	SOS	Did Hap pat? The cup got. I have mud.	pig Kip gum	cut hop mug	to you have	p, u
6	3	SOS	Did the chap? You hop Chad. We have chum.	chad much such	chug chug chum	do has with	/ch/
7	3	SOS	Bob has lit. Rap with Lib. Bud is rich.	bad bid rich	rap bug rug	little too said	b, r
8	4	SOS	The little cat ran. Dan said it too. Fan the hot pan.	fib fun not	Dan fat fog	they was here	f, n
9	4	SOS	Sam got ten men. They did get fed. My peg is here.	get men such	sun Sam hem	about find one	e, s,
10	4	SOS	Did you find cash? The men shut one. Bob hit his shin.	mush shop cash	dash shun shot	she for all	/sh/
11	5	SOS	She got them to sit. This is the big ship. That is for them all.	this that them	than thus then	as he some	/th/ - voiced

Lesson	# of words in dictated sentences	Lesson Format	Sentences for dictation / segmenting	Words for SOS/ cards			Focus phonemes
				Focus CVC	Supplemental CVC	Sight Word	
12	5	SOS	He did wish for cash. Some dog is in bed. The yam is as big.	wit wish yen	yap yam wag	away her that	w, y
13	5	SOS	Val did not with that. That can fix the box. Her fox is a pet.	van box wax	fix vat vet	because his two	v, x
14	6	SOS	Because we can zip it up. His bug had to zig-zag too. Val can fix the two zips.	whiz zed zip	zig zag zax	three come does	z
15	6	SOS	Seth does math in the bath. The path does not look bad. Beth can come in at three.	path bath with	thug path Seth	when down where	/th/ - unvoiced
16	6	SOS	Sam got the vet to quit. When did Seth come down here. Where is the math quiz, Beth?	quit quiz quid	quag quip	how many make	/qu/

SOS to Encode! Part 1   **Common Core Connections**

Lesson #	Kindergarten	First Grade
1-2	RF.K.1.B: words are sequences of letters RF.K.1.D: Recognize upper/lower letters RF.K.2.C: blend and segment onset/rime RF.K.2.D: isolate sounds in CVC RF.K.3.A: 1 to 1 letter-sound correspondence RF.K.3.C: read high frequency words	RF.1.2.B: blend phonemes to produce words RF.1.2.C: isolate sounds in CVC RF.1.2.D: segment phonemes RF.1.3.B: decode one syllable words RF.1.3.G: read irregularly spelled words
3-16	**In addition to above standards:** RF.K.1.A: follow words left-right, top-bottom RF.K.1.C: words separated by spaces	**In addition to above standards:** RF.1.1.A: features of sentence
6, 10-11, 15-16	**In addition to above standards:** (no digraph standards in Kindergarten)	**In addition to above standards:** RF.1.3.A: spell/decode consonant digraphs

Lesson 1: Days 1-2

Date: _____

SOS – Phonemes (5 minutes) 1. Teacher says/shows phoneme 2. Students repeat phoneme 3. If correct, students write letter in sand as they say name 4. Student repeats phoneme and name.	**c, o, a, d**

	cod doc dad	cad dac ad od
SOS- phonetic words (5 minutes) 1. Teacher says/shows word/syllable 2. Students repeat word 3. Students segment the sounds (**finger tap**) 4. Students spell word aloud 5. If correct, students write letters as they say names in sand 6. Student decodes the word.		

SOS – sight words (5 minutes) 1. Teacher says/shows word 2. Students repeat word 3. Students **finger tap** letter names of word and repeat. 4. Students spell word aloud 5. If correct, students write letters as they say names in sand 6. Student reads the word.	a go I

Introduce multisensory sentence segmentation (5 minutes) 1. Teacher says sentence 2. Teacher segments sentence (**table pound**). 3. Students and teacher **table pound** sentence 4. Students **table pound** sentences independently. 5. Repeat with each sentence.	Go doc go! The cat is bad. The dog is mad. We play. We run.

Lesson 1: Days 1-2   Flashcards

Lesson 1

c

Lesson 1

d

Lesson 1

o

Lesson 1

a

Lesson 1

cod

Lesson 1

doc

Lesson 1

cad

Lesson 1

dac

Lesson 1

dad

Lesson 1

doc

Lesson 1

ad

Lesson 1

od

Lesson 1

a

Lesson 1

go

Lesson 1

I

Lesson 1

Go doc go!

Lesson 1

The cat is bad.

Lesson 1

The dog is mad.

Lesson 1

We play. We run.

Lesson 2: Days 3-4

Date: _____

SOS – Phonemes (5 minutes) 1. Teacher says/shows phoneme 2. Students repeat phoneme 3. If correct, students write letter in sand as they say name 4. Student repeats phoneme and name.	**g, m, h, l**

SOS- phonetic words (5 minutes) 1. Teacher says/shows word/syllable 2. Students repeat word 3. Students segment the sounds (**finger tap**) 4. Students spell word aloud 5. If correct, students write letters as they say names in sand 6. Student decodes the word.	dog mad dam	log cog lad hog ham had

SOS – sight words (5 minutes) 1. Teacher says/shows word 2. Students repeat word 3. Students **finger tap** letter names of word and repeat. 4. Students spell word aloud 5. If correct, students write letters as they say names in sand 6. Student reads the word.	see the is

Introduce multisensory sentence segmentation (5 minutes) 1. Teacher says sentence 2. Teacher segments sentence (**table pound**). 3. Students and teacher **table pound** sentence 4. Students **table pound** sentences independently. 5. Repeat with each sentence.	The dog is mad. The house is pretty. I can play outside. They run. They play.

Lesson 2

Lesson 2

g

m

Lesson 2

Lesson 2

h

l

Lesson 2

Lesson 2

dog

mad

Lesson 2

Lesson 2

dam

ham

Lesson 1

Lesson 1

dad

doc

Lesson 2

Lesson 2

log

cod

Lesson 2: Days 3-4   Flashcards continued

Lesson 2

had

Lesson 2

cad

Lesson 2

hog

Lesson 2

is

Lesson 2

see

Lesson 2

the

Lesson 2

The dog is mad.

Lesson 2

The house is pretty.

Lesson 2

I can play outside.

Lesson 2

They run.

Lesson 2

They play.

Lesson 3: Days 5-6

Date: _____

SOS – Phonemes (5 minutes) 1. Teacher says/shows phoneme 2. Students repeat phoneme 3. If correct, students write letter in sand as they say name 4. Student repeats phoneme and name.	**t, i**

	Focus Words:	Supplemental:
SOS- phonetic words (5 minutes) 1. Teacher says/shows word 2. Students repeat word 3. Students segment the sounds 4. Students spell word aloud 5. If correct, students write letters as they say names 6. Student reads the word.	tag Tim hit	lad hog ham

SOS – sight words (5 minutes) 1. Teacher says/shows word 2. Students repeat word 3. Students "tap out" word and repeat. 4. Students spell word aloud 5. If correct, students write letters as they say names 6. Student reads the word. Student reads phrase	and me look
SOS sentences (10-20 minutes) 1. Teacher says/shows sentence 2. Students repeat sentence 3. Students segment/ "pound out" sentence 4. Students "tap out" word/ segment word based on word type 5. Students spell word aloud 6. If correct, students write letters as they say names 7. Student reads the word. 8. Repeat with each word. 9. Student reads sentence 10. Students use COPS with teacher prompting to edit sentence and correct based on model sentence. 11. Repeat with each sentence.	Tom got. Dot had. Tim did.

Lesson 3: Days 5-6   Flashcards

Lesson 3	Lesson 3
t	**i**
Lesson 3	Lesson 3
tag	Tim
Lesson 3	Lesson 3
hit	lad
Lesson 3	Lesson 3
hog	ham
Lesson 3	Lesson 3
and	me
Lesson 3	
look	

Lesson 3

Tom got.

Lesson 3

Dot had.

Lesson 3

Tim did.

Decodable Words

	Write			Rewrite

1. ___   ___   ___   _____

2. ___   ___   ___   _____

3. ___   ___   ___   _____

Sight Words

1. _____   2. _____   3. _____

Sentences

1. △_____   _____☐

_____

2. △_____   _____☐

_____

3. △_____   _____☐

	C △	O big dog	P ☐ . ! ?	S boi or boy
1				
2				
3				

Lesson 4 : Days 7-8

Date: _____

SOS – Phonemes (5 minutes) 1. Teacher says/shows phoneme 2. Students repeat phoneme 3. If correct, students write letter in sand as they say name 4. Student repeats phoneme and name.	**j, k**

SOS- phonetic words (5 minutes) 1. Teacher says/shows word 2. Students repeat word 3. Students segment the sounds 4. Students spell word aloud 5. If correct, students write letters as they say names 6. Student reads the word.	<u>Focus Words:</u> Kim kit jam	<u>Supplemental:</u> Jim jog kid

SOS – sight words (5 minutes) 1. Teacher says/shows word 2. Students repeat word 3. Students "tap out" word and repeat. 4. Students spell word aloud 5. If correct, students write letters as they say names 6. Student reads the word. Student reads phrase	my no play
SOS sentences (10-20 minutes) 1. Teacher says/shows sentence 2. Students repeat sentence 3. Students segment/ "pound out" sentence 4. Students "tap out" word/ segment word based on word type 5. Students spell word aloud 6. If correct, students write letters as they say names 7. Student reads the word. 8. Repeat with each word. 9. Student reads sentence 10. Students use COPS with teacher prompting to edit sentence and correct based on model sentence. 11. Repeat with each sentence.	Jim hid. Kim did. Kid hit.

Lesson 4

j

Lesson 4

k

Lesson 4

Jim

Lesson 4

Kid

Lesson 4

jam

Lesson 4

jog

Lesson 4

Kim

Lesson 4

Kit

Lesson 4

my

Lesson 4

no

Lesson 4

play

Lesson 4

Jim hid.

Lesson 4

Kim did.

Lesson 4

Kid hit.

Decodable Words

Write	Rewrite

1. ___   ___   ___   _____

2. ___   ___   ___   _____

3. ___   ___   ___   _____

Sight Words

1. _____   2._____   3._____

Sentences

1. △ _____   _____ □

_____

2. △ _____   _____ □

_____

3. △ _____   _____ □

	C △	O big dog	P □ . ! ?	S boi or boy
1				
2				
3				

Lesson Plan 5: Days 9-10   Date: _____

SOS – Phonemes (5 minutes) 1. Teacher says/shows phoneme 2. Students repeat phoneme 3. If correct, students write letter in sand as they say name 4. Student repeats phoneme and name.	**p, u**

SOS- phonetic words (5 minutes) 1. Teacher says/shows word 2. Students repeat word 3. Students segment the sounds 4. Students spell word aloud 5. If correct, students write letters as they say names 6. Student reads the word.	Focus Words:	Supplemental:
	pig Kip gum	cut hop mug

SOS – sight words (5 minutes) 1. Teacher says/shows word 2. Students repeat word 3. Students "tap out" word and repeat. 4. Students spell word aloud 5. If correct, students write letters as they say names 6. Student reads the word. Student reads phrase	**to** **you** **have**
SOS sentences (10-20 minutes) 1. Teacher says/shows sentence 2. Students repeat sentence 3. Students segment/ "pound out" sentence 4. Students "tap out" word/ segment word based on word type 5. Students spell word aloud 6. If correct, students write letters as they say names 7. Student reads the word. 8. Repeat with each word. 9. Student reads sentence 10. Students use COPS with teacher prompting to edit sentence and correct based on model sentence. 11. Repeat with each sentence.	**Did Hap pat?** **The cup got.** **I have mud.**

Lesson Plan 5: Days 9-10 Flashcards

Lesson 5

p

Lesson 5

u

Lesson 5

pig

Lesson 5

kip

Lesson 5

cut

Lesson 5

gum

Lesson 5

hop

Lesson 5

mug

Lesson 5

to

Lesson 5

you

Lesson 5

have

Lesson 5

Did Hap pat?

Lesson 5

The cup got.

Lesson 5

I have mud.

Decodable Words

| Write | Rewrite |

1. ____   ____   ____   _____

2. ____   ____   ____   _____

3. ____   ____   ____   _____

Sight Words

1. _____   2._____   3._____

Sentences

1. △_____   _____   _____ □

_____

2. △_____   _____   _____ □

_____

3. △_____   _____   _____ □

_____

	C △	O big dog	P □ . ! ?	S boi or boy
1				
2				
3				

Lesson Plan 6: Days 11-12   Date: _____

SOS – Phonemes (5 minutes) 1. Teacher says/shows phoneme 2. Students repeat phoneme 3. If correct, students write letter in sand as they say name 4. Student repeats phoneme and name.	**ch**

SOS- phonetic words (5 minutes) 1. Teacher says/shows word 2. Students repeat word 3. Students segment the sounds 4. Students spell word aloud 5. If correct, students write letters as they say names 6. Student reads the word.	Focus Words:	Supplemental:
	Ch a d m u ch s u ch	chug chum chup

SOS – sight words (5 minutes) 1. Teacher says/shows word 2. Students repeat word 3. Students "tap out" word and repeat. 4. Students spell word aloud 5. If correct, students write letters as they say names 6. Student reads the word. Student reads phrase	do has with

| **SOS sentences (10-20 minutes)**
1. Teacher says/shows sentence
2. Students repeat sentence
3. Students segment/ "pound out" sentence
4. Students "tap out" word/ segment word based on word type
5. Students spell word aloud
6. If correct, students write letters as they say names
7. Student reads the word.
8. Repeat with each word.
9. Student reads sentence
10. Students use COPS with teacher prompting to edit sentence and correct based on model sentence.
11. Repeat with each sentence. | Did the chap?
You hop Chad.
We have chum. |

Lesson 6

ch

Lesson 6

Chad

Lesson 6

much

Lesson 6

such

Lesson 6

chug

Lesson 6

chup

Lesson 6

chum

Lesson 6

do

Lesson 6

has

Lesson 6

with

Lesson 6

Did the chap?

Lesson 6

You hop Chad.

Lesson 6

We have chum.

Name_____   SOS Sheet   Lesson 6: Days 11-12

Decodable Words

Write	Rewrite

1. ___ ___ ___   _____

2. ___ ___ ___   _____

3. ___ ___ ___   _____

Sight Words

1. _____   2._____   3._____

Sentences

1. △ _____ _____ _____ □

_____

2. △ _____ _____ _____ □

_____

3. △ _____ _____ _____ □

	C △	O big dog	P □ . ! ?	S boi or boy
1				
2				
3				

45

Lesson Plan 7: Days 13-14   Date: _____

SOS – Phonemes (5 minutes) 1. Teacher says/shows phoneme 2. Students repeat phoneme 3. If correct, students write letter in sand as they say name 4. Student repeats phoneme and name.	**b, r**

SOS- phonetic words (5 minutes) 1. Teacher says/shows word 2. Students repeat word 3. Students segment the sounds 4. Students spell word aloud 5. If correct, students write letters as they say names 6. Student reads the word.	Focus Words:	Supplemental:
	<u>b</u> <u>a</u> <u>d</u> <u>r</u> <u>i</u> <u>ch</u> <u>b</u> <u>i</u> <u>d</u>	rap rug bug

SOS – sight words (5 minutes) 1. Teacher says/shows word 2. Students repeat word 3. Students "tap out" word and repeat. 4. Students spell word aloud 5. If correct, students write letters as they say names 6. Student reads the word. Student reads phrase	**little** **too** **said**
SOS sentences (10-20 minutes) 1. Teacher says/shows sentence 2. Students repeat sentence 3. Students segment/ "pound out" sentence 4. Students "tap out" word/ segment word based on word type 5. Students spell word aloud 6. If correct, students write letters as they say names 7. Student reads the word. 8. Repeat with each word. 9. Student reads sentence 10. Students use COPS with teacher prompting to edit sentence and correct based on model sentence. 11. Repeat with each sentence.	**Bob has lit.** **Rap with Lib.** **Bud is rich.**

Lesson 7

Lesson 7

b

r

Lesson 7

Lesson 7

bad

rich

Lesson 7

Lesson 7

bid

rap

Lesson 7

Lesson 7

rug

bug

Lesson 7

Lesson 7

little

too

Lesson 7

said

Lesson 7

Bob has lit.

Lesson 7

Rap with Lib.

Lesson 7

Bud is rich.

Decodable Words

	Write			Rewrite
1.	___	___	___	_____
2.	___	___	___	_____
3.	___	___	___	_____

Sight Words

1. _____   2._____   3._____

Sentences

1. △ _____   _____   _____ □

_____

2. △ _____   _____   _____ □

_____

3. △ _____   _____   _____ □

_____

	C △	O big dog	P □ . ! ?	S boi or boy
1				
2				
3				

Lesson Plan 8: Days 15-16   Date: _____

SOS – Phonemes (5 minutes) 1. Teacher says/shows phoneme 2. Students repeat phoneme 3. If correct, students write letter in sand as they say name 4. Student repeats phoneme and name.	**f, n**
SOS- phonetic words (5 minutes) 1. Teacher says/shows word 2. Students repeat word 3. Students segment the sounds 4. Students spell word aloud 5. If correct, students write letters as they say names 6. Student reads the word.	<table><tr><td>Focus Words:</td><td>Supplemental:</td></tr><tr><td>fib fun not</td><td>Dan fat fog</td></tr></table>
SOS – sight words (5 minutes) 1. Teacher says/shows word 2. Students repeat word 3. Students "tap out" word and repeat. 4. Students spell word aloud 5. If correct, students write letters as they say names 6. Student reads the word. Student reads phrase	**they** **was** **here**
SOS sentences (10-20 minutes) 1. Teacher says/shows sentence 2. Students repeat sentence 3. Students segment/ "pound out" sentence 4. Students "tap out" word/ segment word based on word type 5. Students spell word aloud 6. If correct, students write letters as they say names 7. Student reads the word. 8. Repeat with each word. 9. Student reads sentence 10. Students use COPS with teacher prompting to edit sentence and correct based on model sentence. 11. Repeat with each sentence.	**The little cat ran.** **Dan said it too.** **Fan the hot pan.**

Lesson 8

f

Lesson 8

n

Lesson

fib

Lesson

fun

Lesson

Dan

Lesson

not

Lesson

fat

Lesson

fog

Lesson

they

Lesson

was

Lesson

here

Lesson

The little cat ran.

Lesson

Dan said it too.

Lesson

Fan the hot pan.

Name_____   SOS Sheet   Lesson 8: Days 15-16

Decodable Words

	Write			Rewrite

1. _____ _____ _____   _____

2. _____ _____ _____   _____

3. _____ _____ _____   _____

Sight Words

1. _____   2._____   3._____

Sentences

1. △ _____ _____ _____ _____ □

_____

2. △ _____ _____ _____ _____ □

_____

3. △ _____ _____ _____ _____ □

_____

	C △	O big dog	P □ . ! ?	S boi or boy
1				
2				
3				

Lesson Plan 9: Days 17-18   Date: _____

SOS – Phonemes (5 minutes) 1. Teacher says/shows phoneme 2. Students repeat phoneme 3. If correct, students write letter in sand as they say name 4. Student repeats phoneme and name.	**e, s**

SOS- phonetic words (5 minutes) 1. Teacher says/shows word 2. Students repeat word 3. Students segment the sounds 4. Students spell word aloud 5. If correct, students write letters as they say names 6. Student reads the word.	<u>Focus Words:</u> get men such	<u>Supplemental:</u> sun Sam hem

SOS – sight words (5 minutes) 1. Teacher says/shows word 2. Students repeat word 3. Students "tap out" word and repeat. 4. Students spell word aloud 5. If correct, students write letters as they say names 6. Student reads the word. Student reads phrase	**about** **find** **one**

SOS sentences (10-20 minutes) 1. Teacher says/shows sentence 2. Students repeat sentence 3. Students segment/ "pound out" sentence 4. Students "tap out" word/ segment word based on word type 5. Students spell word aloud 6. If correct, students write letters as they say names 7. Student reads the word. 8. Repeat with each word. 9. Student reads sentence 10. Students use COPS with teacher prompting to edit sentence and correct based on model sentence. 11. Repeat with each sentence.	Sam got ten men. They did get fed. My peg is here.

Lesson Plan 9: Days 17-18   Flashcards

Lesson 9	Lesson 9
e	s
Lesson 9	Lesson 9
get	men
Lesson 9	Lesson 9
such	sun
Lesson 9	Lesson 9
hem	Sam
Lesson 9	Lesson 9
about	one
Lesson 9	
find	

Lesson 9

Sam got ten men.

Lesson 9

They did get fed.

Lesson 9

My peg is here.

Decodable Words

Write	Rewrite
1. ___ ___ ___	_____
2. ___ ___ ___	_____
3. ___ ___ ___	_____

Sight Words

1. _____   2._____   3._____

Sentences

1. △ _____ _____ _____ □

_____

2. △ _____ _____ _____ □

_____

3. △ _____ _____ _____ □

	C △	O big dog	P □ . ! ?	S boi or boy
1				
2				
3				

Lesson Plan 10: Days 19-20   Date: _____

SOS – Phonemes (5 minutes) 1. Teacher says/shows phoneme 2. Students repeat phoneme 3. If correct, students write letter in sand as they say name 4. Student repeats phoneme and name.	## sh

SOS- phonetic words (5 minutes) 1. Teacher says/shows word 2. Students repeat word 3. Students segment the sounds 4. Students spell word aloud 5. If correct, students write letters as they say names 6. Student reads the word.	Focus Words:	Supplemental:
	mush shop cash	shun shot dash

SOS – sight words (5 minutes) 1. Teacher says/shows word 2. Students repeat word 3. Students "tap out" word and repeat. 4. Students spell word aloud 5. If correct, students write letters as they say names 6. Student reads the word. Student reads phrase	she for all
SOS sentences (10-20 minutes) 1. Teacher says/shows sentence 2. Students repeat sentence 3. Students segment/ "pound out" sentence 4. Students "tap out" word/ segment word based on word type 5. Students spell word aloud 6. If correct, students write letters as they say names 7. Student reads the word. 8. Repeat with each word. 9. Student reads sentence 10. Students use COPS with teacher prompting to edit sentence and correct based on model sentence. 11. Repeat with each sentence.	Did you find cash? The men shut one. Bob hit his shin.

Lesson 10

sh

Lesson 10

Lesson 10

mush

shop

Lesson 10

Lesson 10

cash

shun

Lesson 10

Lesson 10

shot

dash

Lesson 10

Lesson 10

she

for

Lesson 10

all

Lesson 10

Did you find cash?

Lesson 10

The men shut one.

Lesson 10

Bob hit his shin.

Decodable Words

Write   Rewrite

1. ___   ___   ___   _____

2. ___   ___   ___   _____

3. ___   ___   ___   _____

Sight Words

1. _____   2._____   3._____

Sentences

1. △ _____ _____ _____ _____ □

_____

2. △ _____ _____ _____ _____ □

_____

3. △ _____ _____ _____ _____ □

_____

	C △	O big dog	P □ . ! ?	S boi or boy
1				
2				
3				

Lesson Plan 11: Days 21-22   Date: _____

SOS – Phonemes (5 minutes) 1. Teacher says/shows phoneme 2. Students repeat phoneme 3. If correct, students write letter in sand as they say name 4. Student repeats phoneme and name.	**/th/ - voiced**

SOS- phonetic words (5 minutes) 1. Teacher says/shows word 2. Students repeat word 3. Students segment the sounds 4. Students spell word aloud 5. If correct, students write letters as they say names 6. Student reads the word.	Focus Words:	Supplemental:
	th i s **th a t** **th e m**	**than** **thus** **then**

SOS – sight words (5 minutes) 1. Teacher says/shows word 2. Students repeat word 3. Students "tap out" word and repeat. 4. Students spell word aloud 5. If correct, students write letters as they say names 6. Student reads the word. Student reads phrase	**as** **he** **some**

SOS sentences (10-20 minutes) 1. Teacher says/shows sentence 2. Students repeat sentence 3. Students segment/ "pound out" sentence 4. Students "tap out" word/ segment word based on word type 5. Students spell word aloud 6. If correct, students write letters as they say names 7. Student reads the word. 8. Repeat with each word. 9. Student reads sentence 10. Students use COPS with teacher prompting to edit sentence and correct based on model sentence. 11. Repeat with each sentence.	**She got them to sit.** **This is the big ship.** **That is for them all.**

Lesson 11

th

Lesson 11

Lesson 11

this

Lesson 11

that

Lesson 11

them

Lesson 11

than

Lesson 11

thus

Lesson 11

then

Lesson 11

as

Lesson 11

he

Lesson 11

some

Lesson 11

She got them to sit.

Lesson 11

This is the big ship.

Lesson 11

That is for them all.

Decodable Words

         Write   Rewrite

1. ___   ___   ___   _____

2. ___   ___   ___   _____

3. ___   ___   ___   _____

Sight Words

1. _____   2._____   3._____

Sentences

1. △ ___ ___ ___ ___ ___ ___ □

    _____

2. △ ___ ___ ___ ___ ___ ___ □

    _____

3. △ ___ ___ ___ ___ ___ ___ □

    _____

	C △	O big dog	P □ . ! ?	S boi or boy
1				
2				
3				

Lesson Plan 12: Days 23-24   Date: _____

SOS – Phonemes (5 minutes) 1. Teacher says/shows phoneme 2. Students repeat phoneme 3. If correct, students write letter in sand as they say name 4. Student repeats phoneme and name.	**W, Y**

| **SOS- phonetic words (5 minutes)**
1. Teacher says/shows word
2. Students repeat word
3. Students segment the sounds
4. Students spell word aloud
5. If correct, students write letters as they say names
6. Student reads the word. | **Focus Words:**
wit
yen
<u>w</u> i <u>sh</u> | **Supplemental:**
yap
wag
yam |

SOS – sight words (5 minutes) 1. Teacher says/shows word 2. Students repeat word 3. Students "tap out" word and repeat. 4. Students spell word aloud 5. If correct, students write letters as they say names 6. Student reads the word. Student reads phrase	**away** **her** **that**
SOS sentences (10-20 minutes) 1. Teacher says/shows sentence 2. Students repeat sentence 3. Students segment/ "pound out" sentence 4. Students "tap out" word/ segment word based on word type 5. Students spell word aloud 6. If correct, students write letters as they say names 7. Student reads the word. 8. Repeat with each word. 9. Student reads sentence 10. Students use COPS with teacher prompting to edit sentence and correct based on model sentence. 11. Repeat with each sentence.	He did wish for cash. Some dog is in bed. The yam is as big.

Lesson Plan 12: Days 23-24   Flashcards

Lesson 12

w

Lesson 12

y

Lesson 12

wit

Lesson 12

yen

Lesson 12

wish

Lesson 12

yap

Lesson 12

wag

Lesson 12

yam

Lesson 12

away

Lesson 12

her

Lesson 12

that

Lesson 12

He did wish for cash.

Lesson 12

Some dog is in bed.

Lesson 12

The yam is as big.

Decodable Words

Write   Rewrite

1. ___ ___ ___   _____

2. ___ ___ ___   _____

3. ___ ___ ___   _____

Sight Words

1. _____   2._____   3._____

Sentences

1. △ ___ ___ ___ ___ ___ □

_____

2. △ ___ ___ ___ ___ ___ □

_____

3. △ ___ ___ ___ ___ ___ □

	C △	O big dog	P □ . ! ?	S boi or boy
1				
2				
3				

Lesson Plan 13: Days 25-26   Date: _____

SOS – Phonemes (5 minutes) 1. Teacher says/shows phoneme 2. Students repeat phoneme 3. If correct, students write letter in sand as they say name 4. Student repeats phoneme and name.	**v, x**

SOS- phonetic words (5 minutes) 1. Teacher says/shows word 2. Students repeat word 3. Students segment the sounds 4. Students spell word aloud 5. If correct, students write letters as they say names 6. Student reads the word.	<u>Focus Words:</u> van box wax	<u>Supplemental:</u> vat vet fix

SOS – sight words (5 minutes) 1. Teacher says/shows word 2. Students repeat word 3. Students "tap out" word and repeat. 4. Students spell word aloud 5. If correct, students write letters as they say names 6. Student reads the word. Student reads phrase	**because** **his** **two**

SOS sentences (10-20 minutes) 1. Teacher says/shows sentence 2. Students repeat sentence 3. Students segment/ "pound out" sentence 4. Students "tap out" word/ segment word based on word type 5. Students spell word aloud 6. If correct, students write letters as they say names 7. Student reads the word. 8. Repeat with each word. 9. Student reads sentence 10. Students use COPS with teacher prompting to edit sentence and correct based on model sentence. 11. Repeat with each sentence.	Val did not with that. That can fix the box. Her fox is a pet.

Lesson Plan 13: Days 25-26   Flashcards

Lesson 13

V

Lesson 13

X

Lesson 13

van

Lesson 13

wax

Lesson 13

box

Lesson 13

vat

Lesson 13

vet

Lesson 13

fix

Lesson 13

because

Lesson 13

his

Lesson 13

too

Lesson 13

Val did not with that.

Lesson 13

That can fix the box.

Lesson 13

Her fox is a pet.

Name_____

Decodable Words

	Write			Rewrite

1. ___ ___ ___   _____

2. ___ ___ ___   _____

3. ___ ___ ___   _____

Sight Words

1. _____   2._____   3._____

Sentences

1. △ _____ _____ _____ _____ _____ □

_____

2. △ _____ _____ _____ _____ _____ □

_____

3. △ _____ _____ _____ _____ _____ □

_____

	C △	O big dog	P □ . ! ?	S boi or boy
1				
2				
3				

Lesson Plan 14: Days 27-28   Date: _____

SOS – Phonemes (5 minutes) 1. Teacher says/shows phoneme 2. Students repeat phoneme 3. If correct, students write letter in sand as they say name 4. Student repeats phoneme and name.	**z**

SOS- phonetic words (5 minutes) 1. Teacher says/shows word 2. Students repeat word 3. Students segment the sounds 4. Students spell word aloud 5. If correct, students write letters as they say names 6. Student reads the word.	<u>Focus Words:</u> **wh i z** zed zip	<u>Supplemental:</u> zig zag zax

SOS – sight words (5 minutes) 1. Teacher says/shows word 2. Students repeat word 3. Students "tap out" word and repeat. 4. Students spell word aloud 5. If correct, students write letters as they say names 6. Student reads the word. Student reads phrase	**three** **come** **does**

SOS sentences (10-20 minutes) 1. Teacher says/shows sentence 2. Students repeat sentence 3. Students segment/ "pound out" sentence 4. Students "tap out" word/ segment word based on word type 5. Students spell word aloud 6. If correct, students write letters as they say names 7. Student reads the word. 8. Repeat with each word. 9. Student reads sentence 10. Students use COPS with teacher prompting to edit sentence and correct based on model sentence. 11. Repeat with each sentence.	Because we can zip it up. His bug had to zig-zag too. Val can fix the two zips.

Lesson 14

z

Lesson 14

whiz

Lesson 14

zed

Lesson 14

zip

Lesson 5

zig

Lesson 14

zag

Lesson 5

zax

Lesson 14

three

Lesson 14

come

Lesson 14

does

Lesson 14

Because we can zip it up.

Lesson 14

His bug had to zig-zag too.

Lesson 14

Val can fix the two zips.

Decodable Words

Write   Rewrite

1. ___ ___ ___   _____

2. ___ ___ ___   _____

3. ___ ___ ___   _____

Sight Words

1. _____   2._____   3._____

Sentences

1. △_____ ___ ___ ___ ___ ___ □

_____

2. △_____ ___ ___ ___ ___ □

_____

3. △_____ ___ ___ ___ ___ □

	C △	O big dog	P □ . ! ?	S boi or boy
1				
2				
3				

Lesson Plan 15: Days 29-30   Date: _____

SOS – Phonemes (5 minutes) 1. Teacher says/shows phoneme 2. Students repeat phoneme 3. If correct, students write letter in sand as they say name 4. Student repeats phoneme and name.	**/th/ - unvoiced**

SOS- phonetic words (5 minutes) 1. Teacher says/shows word 2. Students repeat word 3. Students segment the sounds 4. Students spell word aloud 5. If correct, students write letters as they say names 6. Student reads the word.	**Focus Words:** <u>p</u> <u>a</u> <u>th</u> <u>b</u> <u>a</u> <u>th</u> <u>w</u> <u>i</u> <u>th</u>	**Supplemental:** thug math Seth

SOS – sight words (5 minutes) 1. Teacher says/shows word 2. Students repeat word 3. Students "tap out" word and repeat. 4. Students spell word aloud 5. If correct, students write letters as they say names 6. Student reads the word. Student reads phrase	**when** **down** **where**

SOS sentences (10-20 minutes) 1. Teacher says/shows sentence 2. Students repeat sentence 3. Students segment/ "pound out" sentence 4. Students "tap out" word/ segment word based on word type 5. Students spell word aloud 6. If correct, students write letters as they say names 7. Student reads the word. 8. Repeat with each word. 9. Student reads sentence 10. Students use COPS with teacher prompting to edit sentence and correct based on model sentence. 11. Repeat with each sentence.	Seth does math in the bath. The path does not look bad. Beth can come in at three.

Lesson Plan 15: Days 29-30   Flashcards

Lesson 15

th

Lesson 15

path

Lesson 15

bath

Lesson 15

thug

Lesson 15

with

Lesson 15

math

Lesson 15

Seth

Lesson 15

when

Lesson 15

down

Lesson 15

where

79

Lesson 15

Seth does math in the bath.

Lesson 15

The path does not look bad.

Lesson 15

Beth can come in at three.

Decodable Words

Write	Rewrite

1. ___ ___ ___   _____

2. ___ ___ ___   _____

3. ___ ___ ___   _____

Sight Words

1. _____   2._____   3._____

Sentences

1. △ ___ ___ ___ ___ ___ ___ ___ □

_____

2. △ ___ ___ ___ ___ ___ ___ ___ □

_____

3. △ ___ ___ ___ ___ ___ ___ ___ □

	C △	O big dog	P □ . ! ?	S boi or boy
1				
2				
3				

Lesson Plan 16: Days 31-32   Date: _____

SOS – Phonemes (5 minutes) 1. Teacher says/shows phoneme 2. Students repeat phoneme 3. If correct, students write letter in sand as they say name 4. Student repeats phoneme and name.	**qu**

SOS- phonetic words (5 minutes) 1. Teacher says/shows word 2. Students repeat word 3. Students segment the sounds 4. Students spell word aloud 5. If correct, students write letters as they say names 6. Student reads the word.	Focus Words:	Supplemental:
	qu i t qu i z qu i d	quag quip

SOS – sight words (5 minutes) 1. Teacher says/shows word 2. Students repeat word 3. Students "tap out" word and repeat. 4. Students spell word aloud 5. If correct, students write letters as they say names 6. Student reads the word. Student reads phrase	**how** **many** **make**

SOS sentences (10-20 minutes) 1. Teacher says/shows sentence 2. Students repeat sentence 3. Students segment/ "pound out" sentence 4. Students "tap out" word/ segment word based on word type 5. Students spell word aloud 6. If correct, students write letters as they say names 7. Student reads the word. 8. Repeat with each word. 9. Student reads sentence 10. Students use COPS with teacher prompting to edit sentence and correct based on model sentence. 11. Repeat with each sentence.	Sam got the vet to quit. When did Seth come down here? Where is the math quiz, Beth?

Lesson 16

qu

Lesson 16

quit

Lesson 16

quiz

Lesson 16

quid

Lesson 16

quag

Lesson 16

quip

Lesson 16

how

Lesson 16

many

Lesson 16

make

Lesson 16

Sam got the vet to quit.

Lesson 16

When did Seth come down here?

Lesson 16

Where is the math quiz, Beth?

Name_____

Decodable Words

| Write | Rewrite |

1. ____ ____ ____   _____

2. ____ ____ ____   _____

3. ____ ____ ____   _____

Sight Words

1. _____   2. _____   3. _____

Sentences

1. △ ___ ___ ___ ___ ___ ___ □

_____

2. △ ___ ___ ___ ___ ___ ___ □

_____

3. △ ___ ___ ___ ___ ___ ___ □

	C △	O big dog	P □ . ! ?	S boi or boy
1				
2				
3				

Student Name: _____

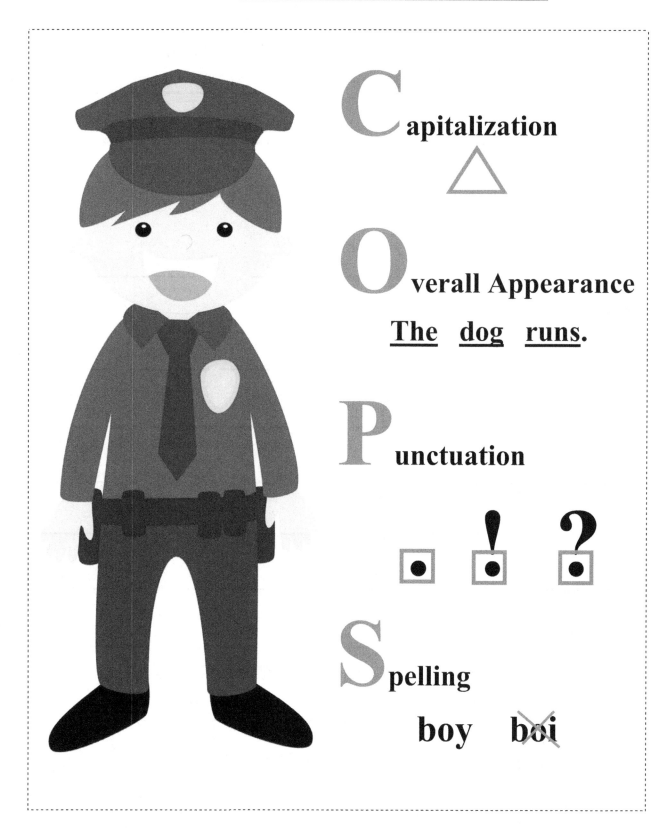

Capitalization

△

Overall Appearance
The dog runs.

Punctuation

! **?**

Spelling

boy ~~boi~~

Sentence Editing Visual: Poster and/or One-Page Sheet for Student Folders
(Linemann & Reid, 2006)

References

Alber-Morgan, S., Hessler, T., & Konra, M. (2007). *Teaching Writing for Keeps.* Education and Treatment of Children, 30, (3). Morgantown, WV: West Virginia University Press.

Benton, E. (1998). *"Ay", "Bee'', "Cee", "One', "Two", "Three" :Using Adaptations of Simultaneous Oral Spelling with Reading-disabled Adults.* Ottawa, Ontario: National Library of Canada.

Bloom, F. & Traub, N. (2005). *Recipe for reading: intervention strategies for struggling readers.* Cambridge and Toronto: Educators Publishing Service.

Boushey, G. & Moser, J. (2006) *The daily 5: fostering literacy independence in the elementary grades.* Portland, ME: Stenhouse Publishers.

Cappello, M., & Moss, B. (2010). *Contemporary Readings in Literacy Education.* Thousand Oaks, CA: Sage Publishing, Inc.

Culham, R. & Avery, C. (2005) *6+1 Traits of Writing: The Complete Guide for the Primary Grades.* New York, NY: Scholastic, Inc.

Gibson, I. (2003). *Teaching Strategies Use to Develop Short Term Memory in Deaf Children.* East Yorkshire, England: British Association of Teachers of the Deaf.

Gillingham, A. & Stillman, B. (1997). *The Gillingham Manual: Remedial training for children with specific disability in reading, spelling, and penmanship.* Cambridge and Toronto: Educators Publishing Service.

Gore, C. (2002). A Study of the Effect of Multisensory Writing Instruction on the Written Expression of the Dyslexic Elementary Child. Baton Rouge, LA: Louisiana State University and Agricultural and Mechanical College.

Kerr, H. (2003). *Consciousness and unconsciousness in teaching and learning: Do we really think too much?* RaPAL Journal 52 20-23.

Lienemann, T. & Reid, R. (2006). *Self-Regulated Strategy Development for Students with Learning Disabilities.* Teacher Education and Special Education. 29,(1), p. 3-11. New York, NY: The H.W. Wilson Company.

Lipson, M. & Wixson, K. (2009). *Assessment and Instruction of Reading and Writing Disabilities*- Fourth Edition, p. 271-274. Boston, MA: Pearson Education, Inc.

Long , L., MacBlain, S., & MacBlain, M. (2007) *Supporting Students with Dyslexia at a Secondary Level: an Emotional Model of Literacy Assessment and Remediation Techniques for Dyslexics.* Journal of Adolescent & Adult Literacy, 51, (2), pp. 124-134. International Reading Association.

MacArthur, C., Graham, C., & Fitzgerald, J. (2006). *Handbook of writing research.* New York, NY: The Guilford Press.

McIntyre, E., Hulan, N., & Layne, V. (2011). *Reading Instruction for Diverse Classrooms.* New York, NY: The Guilford Press.

Mee, M. (1998). *Assessment and Remediation Techniques for Dyslexics.* The English Teacher, 28: Shah Alam, Selangor Darul Ehsa: Pearson Longman

Thank You!

Thank you to From the Pond for the Pond Fonts. Visit the store on Teachers Pay Teachers.
https://www.teacherspayteachers.com/Product/Free-Font-Pond-Free-Me-264977

Thank you to Empty Jar Illustrations for the Police Officer Clipart. Visit the store on Teachers Pay Teachers.
https://www.teacherspayteachers.com/Store/Empty-Jar-Illustrations

Thank you to Creative Clips by Krista Wallden for the great free font! Visit her store on Teachers Pay Teachers.
https://www.teacherspayteachers.com/Store/Krista-Wallden-Creative-Clips

Made in the USA
Middletown, DE
10 June 2020